Usborne
First hundred words
in Spanish

Heather Amery

Illustrated by Stephen Cartwright

Translation and Pronunciation Guide by Jane Straker

Designed by Mike Olley and Jan McCafferty

 There is a little yellow duck to find in every picture.

En el cuarto de estar In the living room

el papá
Daddy

la mamá
Mummy

el niño
boy

About this book

This book is for everyone who is learning their first words in Spanish. By looking at the little pictures, it will be easy to read and remember the Spanish words underneath.

When you look at the Spanish words, you will see that in front of most of them, there is **la** or **el**, which means "the". When you are learning Spanish it is a good idea to learn the **la** or **el** which goes with each one. This is because all words, like book and table, as well as boy and girl, are masculine or feminine. **La** means the word is feminine and **el** usually means that it is masculine. If the word is plural, that is, there is more than one, such as tables or books, then it has **las** or **los** in front of it. **Las** is the feminine and **los** is the masculine.

Some of the words have an n with a squiggle over it, like this **ñ**. The squiggle is called a tilde. In Spanish this **ñ** is a separate letter in the alphabet and is said differently from the ordinary **n**. Some letters have accents on them. This does not change the sound of the letter but changes the way the word is said.

At the back of the book is a guide to help you say all the words in the pictures. But there are some sounds in Spanish which are quite different from any sound in English. To say a Spanish word correctly, you really need to hear a Spanish speaker say it first. Listen very carefully and then try to say it that way yourself. But if you say a word as it is written in the guide, a Spanish person will understand you, even if your Spanish accent is not perfect.

la niña
girl

el bebé
baby

el perro
dog

el gato
cat

3

Vestirse Getting dressed

los zapatos
shoes

la braguita
pants

el jersey
jumper

4

la camiseta
vest

el pantalón
trousers

la camiseta
t-shirt

los
calcetines
socks

En la cocina In the kitchen

el pan
bread

la leche
milk

los huevos
eggs

la manzana
apple

la naranja
orange

el plátano
banana

Lavar los platos

Washing up

la mesa
table

la silla
chair

el plato
plate

8

el cuchillo
knife

el tenedor
fork

la cuchara
spoon

la taza
cup

q

La hora de jugar Play time

el caballo
horse

la oveja
sheep

la vaca
cow

10

la gallina
hen

el cerdo
pig

el tren
train

los cubos
bricks

De visita Going on a visit

la abuela
Granny

el abuelo
Grandpa

las zapatillas
slippers

12

el abrigo
coat

el vestido
dress

el gorro
hat

En el parque In the park

el árbol
tree

la flor
flower

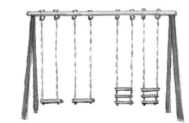

los columpios
swings

el balón
ball

14

el tobogán
slide

las botas
boots

el pájaro
bird

el barco
boat

Por la calle In the street

el coche
car

la bicicleta
bicycle

el avión
plane

la camioneta
truck

el autobús
bus

la casa
house

Celebrar una fiesta
Having a party

el globo
balloon

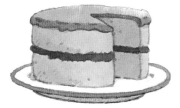

la tarta
cake

el reloj
clock

el helado
ice cream

el pez
fish

las galletas
biscuits

los caramelos
sweets

Nadar Swimming

el brazo
arm

la mano
hand

la pierna
leg

los pies
feet

los dedos
de los pies
toes

la cabeza
head

el trasero
bottom

En el vestuario

In the changing room

la boca
mouth

los ojos
eyes

las orejas
ears

la nariz
nose

el pelo
hair

el peine
comb

el cepillo
brush

23

Ir de compras
Going shopping

rojo
red

azul
blue

verde
green

amarillo
yellow

rosa
pink

blanco
white

negro
black

En el cuarto de baño In the bathroom

el jabón
soap

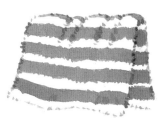

la toalla
towel

el váter
toilet

26

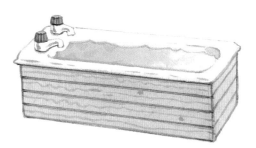

la bañera
bath

la barriguita
tummy

el pato
duck

En el dormitorio In the bedroom

la cama
bed

la lamparilla
lamp

la ventana
window

la puerta
door

el libro
book

la muñeca
doll

el osito
teddy

29

Match the words to the pictures

el balón

las botas

los calcetines

la camiseta

el cerdo

el coche

el cuchillo

el gato

el gorro

el helado

el huevo

el jersey

la lamparilla

la leche

el libro

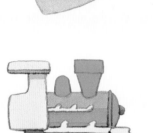

la manzana

la mesa

la muñeca

la naranja

el osito

el pato

el perro

el pez

el plátano

el reloj

la tarta

el tenedor

el tren

la vaca

la ventana

Contar Counting

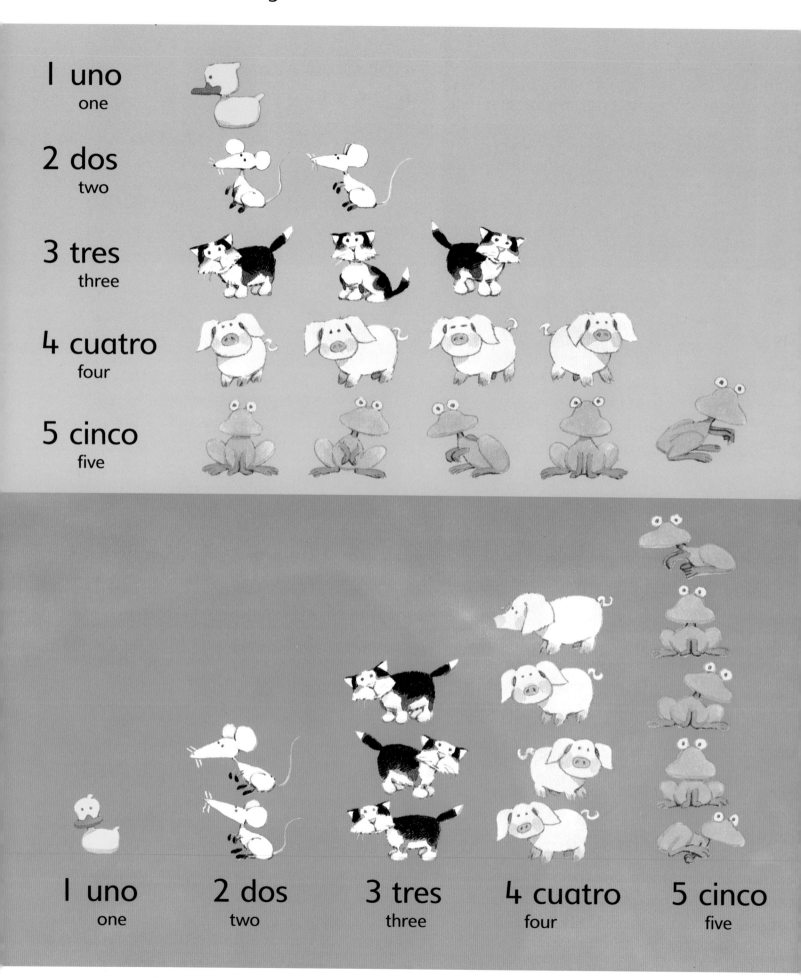

1 uno
one

2 dos
two

3 tres
three

4 cuatro
four

5 cinco
five

1 uno
one

2 dos
two

3 tres
three

4 cuatro
four

5 cinco
five

Words in the pictures

In this alphabetical list of all the words in the pictures, the Spanish word comes first, next is the guide to saying the word, and then there is the English translation. The guide may look strange or funny, but just try to read it as if it were English words. It will help you to say the words in Spanish correctly, if you remember these rules:

Capital, or BIG, letters show which part of the word to stress:

a is said like **a** in h**a**ppen

e is said like **e** in h**e**lp

o is said like **o** in h**o**rse

ch is quite different from any sound in the English language but it is said like the **ch** in the Scottish word lo**ch**

rrr is **r** rolled on your tongue, like the **r** in the name of the Scottish poet Bu**r**ns

th is said like the **th** in mon**th**

abrigo	*aBREEgo*	coat	celebrar	*theleBRAR*	celebrate
abuela	*aBWEla*	Granny	cepillo	*thePEELyo*	brush
abuelo	*aBWElo*	Grandpa	cerdo	*THERdo*	pig
amarillo	*amaREELyo*	yellow	cinco	*THEENko*	five
árbol	*ARbol*	tree	cocina	*koTHEEna*	kitchen
autobús	*aootoBOOSS*	bus	coche	*KOTshe*	car
avión	*abeeONN*	plane	columpios	*koLOOMpyoss*	swings
azul	*aTHOOL*	blue	compras	*KOMprass*	shopping
			contar	*konTAR*	counting
balón	*baLONN*	ball	cuarto de baño	*kwartodeBANyo*	bathroom
bañera	*baNYEra*	bath	cuarto de estar	*kwartodessTAR*	living
barco	*BARko*	boat			room
barriguita	*barrreeGEEta*	tummy	cuatro	*KWAtro*	four
bebé	*beBE*	baby	cubos	*KOOboss*	bricks
bicicleta	*beetheeKLEta*	bicycle	cuchara	*kootSHAra*	spoon
blanco	*BLANko*	white	cuchillo	*kootSHEELyo*	knife
boca	*BOka*	mouth			
botas	*BOtass*	boots	dedos de los pies	*dedoss-delossPYESS*	toes
braguita	*braGEEta*	pants	dormitorio	*dormeeTORyo*	bedroom
brazo	*BRAtho*	arm	dos	*doss*	two
caballo	*kaBALyo*	horse	fiesta	*FYESSta*	party
cabeza	*caBEtha*	head	flor	*flor*	flower
calcetines	*kaltheTEEness*	socks			
calle	*KALye*	street	galletas	*galYEtass*	biscuits
cama	*KAma*	bed	gallina	*galYEEna*	hen
camioneta	*kameeoNEta*	truck	gato	*GAto*	cat
camiseta	*kameeSSEta*	vest, t-shirt	globo	*GLObo*	balloon
caramelos	*karaMEloss*	sweets	gorro	*GOrrro*	hat
casa	*KAssa*	house			

33

Spanish	Pronunciation	English
helado	*eLAdo*	ice cream
hora	*Ora*	time
huevos	*WEboss*	eggs
jabón	*chaBONN*	soap
jersey	*cherSSEY*	jumper
jugar	*chooGAR*	play
lamparilla	*lampaREELya*	light
lavar	*laBAR*	wash
leche	*LETshe*	milk
libro	*LEEbro*	book
mamá	*maMA*	Mummy
mano	*MAno*	hand
manzana	*manTHAna*	apple
mesa	*MEssa*	table
muñeca	*mooNYEka*	doll
nadar	*naDAR*	swimming
naranja	*naRANcha*	orange
nariz	*naREETH*	nose
negro	*NEgro*	black
niña	*NEENya*	girl
niño	*NEENyo*	boy
ojos	*ochos*	eyes
orejas	*oREchas*	ears
osito	*oSEEto*	teddy
oveja	*oBEcha*	sheep
pájaro	*PAcharo*	bird
pan	*pann*	bread
pantalón	*pantaLONN*	trousers
papá	*paPA*	Daddy
parque	*PARke*	park
pato	*PAto*	duck
peine	*PEYne*	comb
pelo	*PElo*	hair
perro	*PErrro*	dog
pez	*peth*	fish
pierna	*PYERna*	leg
pies	*pyess*	feet
plátano	*PLAtano*	banana
plato	*PLAto*	plate
puerta	*PWERta*	door
reloj	*rrreLOCH*	clock
rojo	*RRROcho*	red
rosa	*ROssa*	pink
silla	*SSEELya*	chair
tarta	*TARta*	cake
taza	*TAtha*	cup
tenedor	*teneDOR*	fork
toalla	*toALya*	towel
tobogán	*toboGANN*	slide
trasero	*trassERo*	bottom
tren	*trenn*	train
tres	*tress*	three
uno	*OOno*	one
vaca	*BAka*	cow
váter	*BAter*	toilet
ventana	*benTAna*	window
verde	*BERde*	green
vestido	*besTEEdo*	dress
vestirse	*besTEERse*	getting dressed
vestuario	*bestooAReeo*	changing room
visita	*beeSEEta*	visit
zapatillas	*thapaTEELyas*	slippers
zapatos	*thaPAtoss*	shoes

This edition first published in 2002 by Usborne Publishing Ltd, Usborne House, 83-85 Saffron Hill, London EC1N 8RT, England.
www.usborne.com